Top 10 Worst

Things about Ancient Rome

you wouldn't want to know!

iSalute

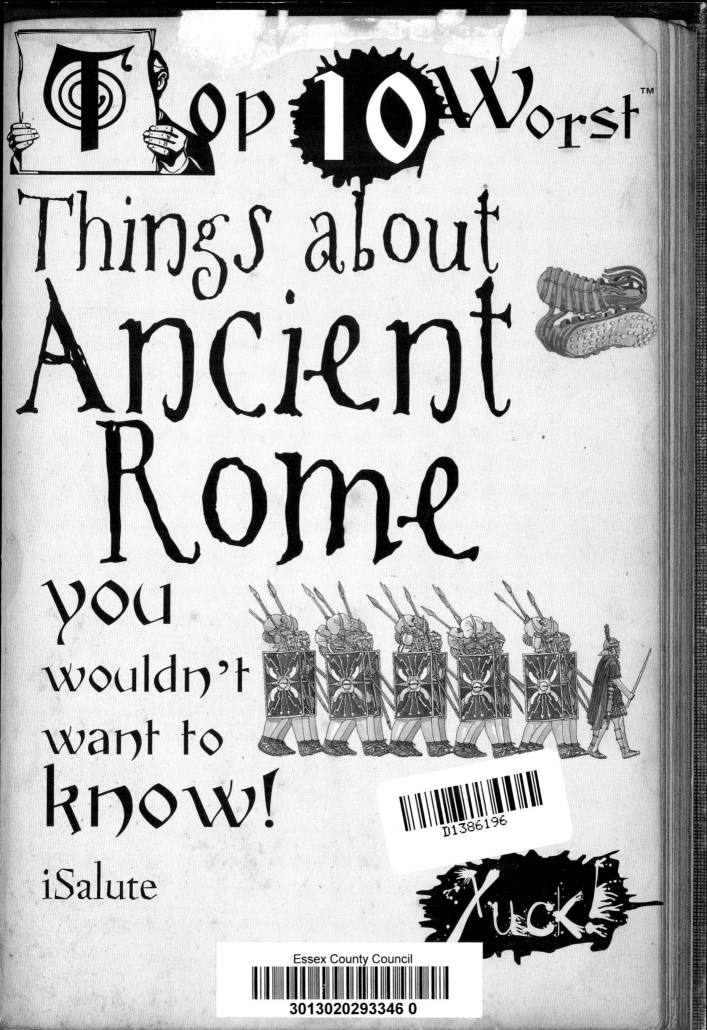

Yuck!

Author:
Victoria England was born in Bath, England. She studied English Literature at the University of Brighton and now lives and works in Brighton.

Artist:
David Antram was born in Brighton, England, in 1958. He studied at Eastbourne College of Art and then worked in advertising for fifteen years before becoming a full-time artist. He has illustrated many children's non-fiction books.

Series creator:
David Salariya was born in Dundee, Scotland. He has illustrated a wide range of books and has created and designed many new series for publishers in the UK and overseas. In 1989 he established The Salariya Book Company. He lives in Brighton with his wife, illustrator Shirley Willis, and their son Jonathan.

Additional artwork: Mark Bergin, John James

Editorial assistants: Rob Walker, Mark Williams

Published in Great Britain in MMXII by
Book House, an imprint of
The Salariya Book Company Ltd
25 Marlborough Place, Brighton BN1 1UB
www.salariya.com
www.book-house.co.uk

HB ISBN-13: 978-1-908177-26-1
PB ISBN-13: 978-1-908177-27-8

SALARIYA

1 3 5 7 9 8 6 4 2
A CIP catalogue record for this book is available from the British Library.

Printed and bound in China.

PAPER FROM
SUSTAINABLE FORESTS

@bookhousebooks The Salariya Book Company BookHouse100

FIND OUR BOOKS
ON THE APP STORE:
SEARCH FOR 'SALARIYA'

Top 10 Worst

Things about

Ancient Rome

you wouldn't want to know!

iSalute

Xuck!

Illustrated by
David Antram

BOOK HOUSE

Created & designed by
David Salariya

Written by
Victoria England

Top 10 Worst things about ancient Rome

Contents

Where in the world?

At its height, the Roman empire covered about 30 present-day countries and had some 50 million people living within its borders. The empire stretched from Britain in the west to Syria in the east, and from Germany in the north to Tunisia in the south. Rome was a superpower and master of the lands around the Mediterranean Sea, but what were the worst things about living in ancient Rome?

The Roman Empire

BRITANNIA

Londinium

GERMANIA

Northern horsemen

Wheat

Prisoners of war

Bees

Skins

Military fort

Honey

BLACK SEA

HISPANIA

ITALIA

Wine

Rome

Olive oil

MEDITERRANEAN SEA

GRAECIA

Papyrus

AFRICA

AEGYPTUS

Date palms

The Roman Empire

The city of Rome was the capital of the empire, the biggest, grandest and busiest city in the Roman world. In AD 64, during Nero's reign, the city was devastated by fire. It was rebuilt and enlarged, but it was not until AD 271 that a strong defensive wall was built. This was called the Aurelian Wall.

City and country

Many Romans lived in large, crowded cities throughout the empire. The great majority, however, lived and worked in the countryside, mostly as poor farmers. Others worked on the estates of rich landowners, who lived in the cities and visited their estates occasionally. The main crops were olives, grapes and grain – the staple ingredients of the Roman diet.

Language

Many different languages were spoken thoughout the Roman empire, but the official language was Latin. This was important in bringing some unity to the various parts of the empire. Educated Romans also learnt Greek. Latin is still studied today and is the official language of the Roman Catholic Church. Here are a few words to start you off:

A Roman villa in the northern part of the empire

Rich and poor

There were far more poor families than rich ones, and the contrasts between them were very great. Rich Romans led pleasant lives, with lovely homes, good food, fine clothes and plenty of slaves to wait on them. If you were poor, however, you had to work hard for your living, scrimp and save money, and do everything for yourself.

Salve! (Hello)

Vale! (Goodbye)

O me miserum! (Woe is me!)

Life in ancient Rome

On the roads

The Romans' huge road system covered 85,000 kilometres. Roads were built quickly so that the army could move from place to place, but civilians benefited too. The army kept the roads safe and there were even guide books available, giving lists of places to stay and road maps. Merchants took advantage of the improved communications, so trade with the provinces flourished.

The roads formed a vital network across the Roman empire.

Only the rich had funerals. The body was carried to the grave in a litter along a path lined with tombstones.

Litter

Death and funerals

More than death itself, rich Romans feared dying unmourned and unburied. Many people arranged and paid for their funerals in advance. People thought the best way to die was surrounded by their family.

The first grapes of the year were picked on 19th August, and a lamb was sacrificed to the gods.

Mount Vesuvius

Baa!

The clothes people wore showed their rank in society – Romans were very status conscious. Boys under 14 (if they were citizens' sons) wore a toga with a purple stripe. At 14 they wore a pure white toga. The emperor's toga was purple. Wealthy women wore a long robe over a tunic, with a shawl, called a palla, draped over their head and shoulders.

Desiste! (Stop it!)

On your guard, Titus!

What's in a name?

A Roman baby was named at a ceremony nine days after its birth. Many Romans had at least two names, a personal name and their family name. Some Roman first names may sound familiar:

- For girls: Julia, Livia, Drusilla, Antonia or Claudia

- For boys: Marcus, Julius, Antonius, Titus, Caius, Didius, Marius or Septimius.

9

№ 10

Home comforts

Most homes didn't have a toilet. Poor familes used big pottery jars instead! In Roman latrines, washable sponge sticks were shared because toilet paper was unknown!

In a big city like Rome the sort of house people lived in depended very much on whether they were rich or poor. The poor people lived in cramped, dingy, high-rise blocks of flats. In general, the higher the storey, the smaller and pokier the flat. Because living space was in short supply, blocks of flats were built higher and higher to cram more people in – and make the landlords richer!

Blocks of flats were known as insulae *(islands) because each one was like a separate community.*

Be prepared!
Always expect the very worst

Living conditions

Flats were built from timber and sun-dried mud and they often fell down. They caught fire too, because people used to keep warm by huddling around clay pots full of burning charcoal. Emperor Augustus passed a law forbidding any new building to be more than 20 metres high.

Bath time

Only rich people had baths in their homes. Most people used the communal public baths to wash. There were four separate stages to taking a bath Roman-style:

• A very hot room full of steam

• A hot, dry room where a slave removed all the sweat and dirt from your skin using a metal scraper and olive oil

• To cool off, a swim in a tepid pool

• A jump into a bracing cold pool!

Most romans only visited the baths an average of once in every nine days!

On the streets

Poor people had to walk everywhere as they could not afford a horse, donkey or carriage. If they were lucky they might have been able to hitch a lift from a farm wagon – but this would not have given them a comfortable ride! The streets were crowded and very dirty and people had to use stepping-stones to avoid the mud and rubbish underfoot.

I paid a slave to look after my clothes.

Let's hope he's honest – I had to run home naked when my clothes were stolen.

No 9

Gods, religion and superstition

The ancient Romans believed in many different gods and goddesses. These were split into two groups. Roman homes were protected by household gods – the *lares* and the *penates*. The gods in the second group were those of the official state religion. People feared these gods and tried to keep them happy with offerings and sacrifices. If things went wrong, they believed it was because the gods were angry.

Eastern cults

Some Roman soldiers found the state religion too stuffy and impersonal and turned instead to cults from the east. Some promised their followers life after death. They were regarded with suspicion by officers because they encouraged non-Roman behaviour, lessening their loyalty to Rome and its emperors.

Mars

Venus

Juno

Jupiter

Jupiter is the king of the gods and Juno his wife. His daughter Venus is the goddess of love and his son Mars is the god of war.

Be prepared!
Always expect the very worst

Symbols of good and evil

• Balding men may stop their hair falling out by sniffing cyclamen flowers!

• The sound of bells is thought to ease a woman's pain in childbirth.

• Bees are sacred messengers of the gods and symbols of good luck.

• Peony flowers have special, magical powers of healing the sick and ill.

• Eagles, emblems of the Roman legions, are said to bring thunderstorms.

Cursed enemies!

Romans often asked the gods to curse their enemies. They wrote their enemies' names, plus curse words, on scraps of metal or pottery and left them at temples. They hoped that the gods would see these messages, and harm the people named in them.

Christianity banned!

Some of the world's first Christians lived in Rome. But until AD 313 Christianity was banned in the Roman Empire. Christians met secretly, in underground passages called catacombs, to say prayers and hold services. They also used the catacombs as a burial place.

A hooting owl foretold danger!

Hooot!

After an animal had been sacrificed to the gods, a priest, called a haruspex, *examined its liver. If it was diseased, bad luck was on the way!*

No 8

feasts and riots

A lthough the Romans enjoyed strong-flavoured, spicy food, poor people could only afford to eat very simple foods, such as soups made with lentils and onions, barley porridge, peas, cabbage and tough, cheap cuts of meat stewed in vinegar. There was no tea or coffee; people drank wine or water instead. It was considered bad manners to drink wine undiluted.

fast food

Only rich people had their own kitchen because they could afford slaves to help. Ordinary people went to *popinae* (cheap eating houses) for their main evening meal, or bought ready-cooked snacks from roadside fast food stalls.

flamingo with dates

Fast-food shops were called thermopolia.

1 Cook flamingo

2 Season water

3 Add dates

4 Pour over flamingo

14

Be prepared!
Always expect the very worst

Government grain

Around half of the population could not earn enough money to buy food. They relied on free grain from the government to avoid starvation. When harvests failed and grain supplies ran short, the citizens who relied on free food rioted outside the government buildings.

Red wine

Pulses

feast with a gladiator

On the night before the games the emperor would arrange a lavish feast and invite all the gladiators. Some would eat little, so they would be alert the next day. Others ate greedily, knowing it might be their last meal. The Romans who were invited to this unpleasant feast with the gladiators enjoyed the knowledge that many of their fellow diners might be dead the next day.

Getting sick at supper

At the best banquets, many guests ate too much of the wonderful food and still wanted more. To solve the problem they would make themselves vomit and then return to the table to eat again!

Wealthy Romans didn't sit up at a table. Instead, they lay propped up on their elbows on long wooden couches. This gave them indigestion.

15

No 7

Sickness and health

Doctors were available for ancient Romans, but they were expensive so many people opted for a local chemist or spent the night in the temple of Aesculapius, the god of healing. Doctors usually treated illnesses with herbal medicines, such as a mustard gargle for a stomach ulcer. They also carried out operations using wine as an anaesthetic!

Battle wounds

Army doctors were highly respected and were assisted by dressers, who treated wounds during battles and nursed the soldiers back to health. Common battle wounds included jagged sword cuts, broken bones and dislocated joints. Sometimes damaged limbs had to be amputated. Salt, arsenic and turpentine were used as antiseptics and kept wounds from becoming infected.

16

Be prepared!
Always expect the very worst

Bewitching illnesses

Despite their advanced technology, Romans believed that illness could be caused by witchcraft. To find a cure, they gave presents to the witch, begging her to remove the spell, or made a special visit to a temple to ask the gods to make them better.

A hospital in a Roman fort.

Injured soldiers bandaged their wounds with cobwebs soaked in vinegar. This helped the soldiers but wasn't so good for the spiders!

Demon barbers

Going to the barber's could be very painful. Barbers used shears to trim men's hair and beards. When a smooth, close-shaven look was in fashion, barbers had to pull men's beards out by the roots, one hair at a time!

1
2
4
5
3
6

1. Spatula (knife for spreading ointment)
2. Tweezers
3. Probe used for shallow wounds
4. Hook
5. Knife used for surgery
6. Forceps

Cured by cabbage?

Cabbage was one of the most popular plant remedies. It was crushed and spread on bruises and boils; stewed for headaches; fried in hot fat to treat sleeplessness; dried, powdered and sniffed to clear blocked noses; and squeezed to extract juice to use as ear drops!*

No 6

Life in the army

A soldier's life was brutal. They might die in battle or from diseases caught on campaign. *Grrr!* Even when they were not fighting, they spent long hours training or building roads and forts. Their food was simple and their discipline harsh. Each legion had about 5,000 soldiers, divided into smaller units of 80 men, called centuries.

Army discipline

Army discipline was ferocious. Men who ran away or disobeyed orders were killed. One commander even executed his own son. Savage punishments like 'decimation' forced soldiers to behave. If just one man in a cohort (unit of 500 soldiers) broke the rules, one in every ten was killed, even though most of them had done nothing wrong!

The Romans liked to collect their enemies' heads as trophies.

Now I'm in the army, I may never see my homeland again!

Be prepared!
Always expect the very worst

Left! Right! Left!

Left, right, left, right!

Marching made the legionaries strong and fit. They had to cover distances of 20 miles (32 km) at a quick pace in five hours. The soldiers were nicknamed 'Marius's mules', after a famous general, because they had to march with all their equipment on their backs.

Sandals had heavy studs on the soles to prevent the leather from wearing down quickly.

Great load

Each soldier had to march carrying his armour, weapons, helmet, shield, cloak, leather bottle (for water or wine), cooking pot, metal dish, spade and mattock (for digging defensive ditches), first-aid kit and two weeks' food. All this weighed over 40 kg!

Hmph! This week my duties include cleaning all the centurions' boots!

I'm cleaning the latrines all week!

The mess room

Eight men were supposed to share each pair of mess rooms. The rooms were cramped and gloomy places to live. One room was used for sleeping, and the other was for storing, cleaning and repairing equipment. All the soldiers had to cook, eat and relax there together.

No 5

Roman rulers

Over the years, Rome was ruled in three different ways: first by kings, then by a number of officials who were chosen by the people, and finally by emperors, who were really kings under a different name! Some Roman emperors ruled wisely, but others were truly dreadful...

Julius Caesar

In 47 BC, a successful general called Julius Caesar declared himself dictator. Many people feared that he was trying to end the republic, and rule like the old kings. Caesar was murdered in 44 BC by a group of his political enemies, including his old friend Marcus Brutus. After this, there were many years of civil war.

Be prepared!
Always expect the very worst

Caligula's rule

Who, me?

Caligula wasted the riches of Rome. He believed he was a god and dressed up as Apollo, Venus, Mercury and Hercules. He exiled his own wife and outraged senators when he insisted on having his horse elected consul and priest – one of the highest political positions!

The madness of Nero

The Emperor Nero was mad and bad. He was said to have laughed and played music while watching a terrible fire that destroyed a large part of Rome. He also tried to kill his own mother by having her ship sunk, but when that failed he simply ordered her to be executed.

More of the worst...

Other rotten rulers included:

- Commodus – adored killing animals and was very lazy.

- Domitian – developed new tortures and killed politicians and wealthy citizens.

- Septimius Severus – persecuted all foreign religions.

- Diocletian – condemned many Christians to be killed by lions in the Colosseum (see page 25).

Emperors through time

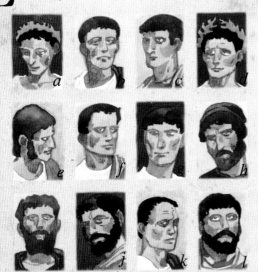

a. **Augustus** (27 BC–AD 14), b. **Tiberius** (AD 14–37), c. **Caligula** (AD 37–41), d. **Claudius** (AD 41–54), e. **Nero** (AD 54–68), f. **Domitian** (AD 81–96), g. **Trajan** (AD 98–117), h. **Hadrian** (AD 117–138), i. **Septimius Severus** (AD 193–211), j. **Caracalla** (AD 211–217), k. **Diocletian** (AD 284–305), l. **Julian the Apostate** (AD 360–363).

No 4

Crime and punishment

The Romans were proud of their laws. They were strict but fair, and everyone was considered innocent until they had been proven guilty in an open trial. However, like any big city, plenty of crimes were still committed in Rome and it was not particularly safe to walk the streets at night for fear of being robbed.

Beware of the dog

Wealthy Romans had bars on their windows, or guard dogs, to deter would-be house burglars. Some houses had the Roman equivalent of 'Beware of the Dog' signs – mosaics with the words CAVE CANEM.

WOOF!

WOOF!

22

The basilica was the largest building in any Roman town or city.

Tax collectors made sure people paid what they owed to the government.

Be prepared!
Always expect the very worst

Death penalty

In the most serious cases of desertion, mutiny or failing to obey orders, the punishment was execution. Some criminals were beheaded; some beaten to death; others were crucified on a wooden cross.

Army punishments

Other army punishments included:

- Pay could be deducted if a unit had appeared cowardly in battle. Soldiers could be put on half pay for a year for serious offences.

- A reduction in rank could be imposed on an officer who had deserted or mutinied.

- Extra duties were imposed for more minor offences. These had to be done in addition to the normal range of duties and included cleaning the latrines. Yuck!

- Soldiers guilty of a minor offence might be made to stand all day holding a pole!

father knows best!

A Roman father had the power of life and death over his family. The *paterfamilias* (father of the family) was usually the oldest surviving male. He had the right to punish any family members who misbehaved. Even his mother and older female relatives were expected to obey him.

23

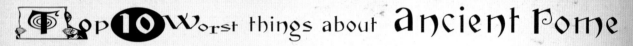

No 3

Gladiator fights!

Ancient Romans admired gladiators for their strength, bravery and skill. However, gladiators' lives were short and their deaths were horrible. They were sent to the arena to fight – and suffer – until they died. On average, half the gladiators involved in any particular fight were likely to be killed.

Beg for mercy

Defeated gladiators raised a finger of the left hand, to show they were begging the emperor for mercy. If he gave the thumbs up signal, they lived. If he turned his thumb downwards, they were killed by a slave dressed as Pluto, the god of the underworld. He would hit them on the forehead with a hammer.

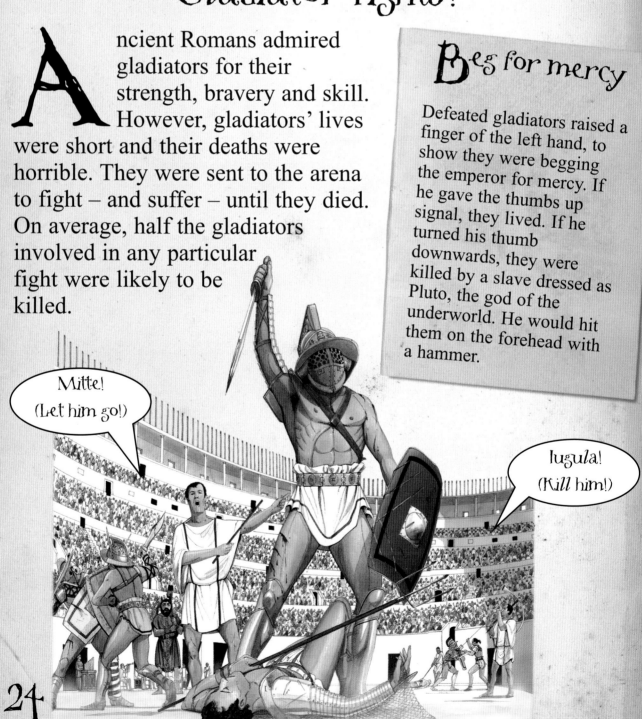

24

Be prepared!
Always expect the very worst

Why become a gladiator?

Some men had no choice. Trainers bought them at the slave market because they looked strong and fit for fighting. The slave-gladiators were kept locked up like prisoners and had to fight at their trainer's command. Some poor young men joined a trainer's team because it seemed the only alternative to starvation.

Chariot racing

Chariots often collided and overturned. Each charioteer carried a sharp knife, called a *falx*, to cut himself free from the wreckage. Even so, many horses and charioteers were killed.

Emperor Trajan held the biggest games at the Colosseum in AD 107: more than 10,000 gladiators fought and 11,000 animals died.

Wild beasts

Hunting was one of the Romans' most popular sports. But, of course, this was not possible in the city of Rome. Fierce wild animals were brought from distant parts of the Roman empire to be killed by gladiators. So many lions were taken from North Africa that they became extinct there.

No 2

Life and death in Pompeii

P ompeii was a bustling town not far from Rome, in the south of Italy. In the year AD 79, a nearby volcano erupted, and buried the town in ash. Pompeii lay hidden for centuries until, one day, some farmers discovered its Roman remains...

Warning signs

In AD 62 an earthquake rocked Pompeii and the countryside around. As the ground shook, statues and buildings wobbled until they cracked and fell. This was a warning sign from Mount Vesuvius. By AD 79, life had returned to normal for the people of Pompeii, until they started to notice lots of odd things...

Strong shakes were felt; cups and plates got broken.

Loud booming noises came from under the ground.

Wells and springs dried up.

The River Sarno was full of dead fish.

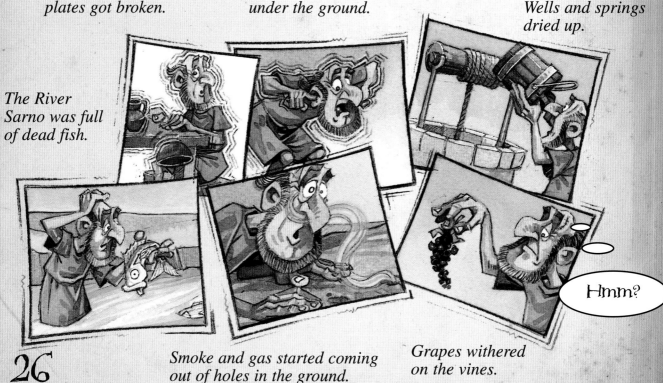

Hmm?

Smoke and gas started coming out of holes in the ground.

Grapes withered on the vines.

Be prepared!
Always expect the very worst

Aaah!

Panic in Pompeii!

- The people of Pompeii gathered up their belongings and tried to leave town.

- Some people seized the chance to steal from the empty houses.

- From late afternoon roofs caved in under the weight of the pumice.

- Pumice floats, and it soon clogged up the River Sarno.

- The choking smell of rotten eggs in the air increased and it became harder to breathe.

Death of a town

In AD 79 millions of tonnes of red-hot volcanic debris surged down the mountain at great speed, quickly reaching the town wall. It was all over in just 30 minutes. Pompeii, the town that 15,000 people had called home, was buried beneath a deep layer of ash.

Pompeii uncovered

In the 1860s, Giuseppe Fiorelli poured plaster into hollowed areas in the ash where bodies had lain.

The modern story of Pompeii begins in 1748, when treasure-hunters began the first of many excavations to find valuable objects. Today, Pompeii is a Roman time capsule, and as visitors walk along the ancient streets and look into shops and houses, it's as if they have been transported back in time to AD 79.

Lost in AD 79 …

… and found almost 2,000 years later!

27

No 1

Slave labour

Slaves for sale!

Roman people were not all equal. There were different classes within Roman society. Throughout the Roman empire, the biggest difference between people was whether they were slaves or free. Slaves belonged to their owners just like dogs or horses.

Slave markets

Slaves were kidnapped in far lands and auctioned at the slave markets. Some were captured in Spain or Greece as prisoners of war. Some had been taken prisoner around the Black Sea or in the eastern Mediterranean, and sold by pirates. As time went on, most slaves were the children of slave parents.

Smack!

When slaves grew more costly, ruthless Roman landowners waylaid passing travellers to make slaves of them.

Slaves were at the bottom of the social pyramid. The settled order of Roman life was dependent on its slave workforce.

Be prepared!
Always expect the very worst

Punishments

Slaves were completely in the power of their owners. If they misbehaved, they were beaten, imprisoned, burned with an iron or sometimes even killed. If a slave killed his master, all of the slaves in the household were put to death!

Working in chains was a punishment for troublesome slaves.

Slaves working for the Colosseum management had to remove the dead bodies.

Yuck!

How to manage slaves

Pay for freedom

Generous owners did give their slaves allowances of money. However, to buy their freedom slaves would have to raise the same sum of money that their master had paid for them – a virtually impossible task.

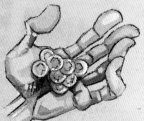

• Put them to work in gangs of no more than ten, so that they are easy to control.

• When buying slaves, avoid those that are too timid or too boisterous.

• Do not have too many slaves of the same nationality, as this leads to squabbles.

• Give the unhealthy work to hired gangs. Do not risk the expensive slaves getting ill.

Glossary

Anaesthetic A drug which causes numbness in the body or a loss of consciousness.

Basilica A large public building, used as a meeting place for merchants, and as the town hall and law court.

Centurion The officer in charge of a century of men in either a legion or an auxiliary unit.

Century A division of men in the Roman army, normally 80 strong, commanded by a centurion.

Charcoal Partly burned wood, used as a fuel.

Citizen A Roman who had the right to vote to elect people to the Senate and to political posts in the Senate. He also had the right to wear a toga and serve as a legionary in the army.

Consul One of two men who headed the government for a one-year term, managing the senate's affairs and commanding the army.

Decimation Executing one tenth of an army.

Desertion Leaving one's duty or failing to carry it out.

Dictator A ruler who has total authority.

Emperor The ruler of an empire. Usually had tremendous personal power.

Estate A villa and all the farmland belonging to it.

Excavation The process of digging into the ground to look for remains of past civilisations.

Imperial Belonging to an empire.

Imperial times The period when Romans were ruled by emperors, from 27 BC to the fall of the western Roman empire in AD 476.

Insula A block of flats or group of buildings. The word initially meant 'island'.

Lares The household gods.

Legion One of approximately 30 units of men, recruited from Roman citizens, who were the best-trained and most feared soldiers in the Roman empire.

Litter A form of transport: a lightweight portable bed carried shoulder-high by slaves.

Mattock A digging tool, with a blade at right angles to the handle.

Mosaic A decorative surface for floors and walls made by setting tiny cubes of coloured stone or glass into mortar.

Mutiny Rebellion against officers.

Palla A woollen shawl worn by Roman women in cold weather.

Paterfamilias The head of the household; the father of the family.

Province An area outside Rome that was under Roman control. The rest of Italy was considered to be a province of Rome.

Pumice A lightweight stone, formed from cooled volcanic lava.

Republic A country that is not ruled by a king or emperor but is governed by a group of officials elected by the people.

Republican times From the founding of the Roman republic in 509 BC to the beginning of the reign of Augustus in 27 BC.

Sacrifice A living creature that is killed in order to please or calm the gods.

Senator A member of the Senate, the council which ruled Rome during the Republic. The Senate survived into the Imperial period but its powers were much reduced.

Thermopolium (plural **thermopolia**) A shop where poorer Romans could buy hot meals.

Toga A garment worn by men and boys. Made from a semicircular piece of cloth, three times as long as the man was tall.

Turpentine A mixture of oil and resin from pine and other related trees.

Underworld (also known as Hades). The place where a dead person's spirit was thought to go to be judged, before going on to Elysium (heaven) or Tartarus (hell).

Villa A large country house and the farmland surrounding it. Many villa owners also had houses in town.

Index